America's National Parks

A Photographic Tour of All 61 National Parks of the USA

Table of Contents

Acadia National Park is the easternmost National park and occupies the majority of an island off the coast of Maine. With over 150 miles of hiking trails, wildlife like bears, whales, and birds, and beautiful vistas, a visit to Acadia will certainly have something to please any visitor.

Photo Credit: Kim Carpenter

4

Arches National Park, located in Utah, is home to more than 2,000 naturally occurring sandstone formations. At less than 120 square miles, it is a smaller park, but still boasts over a dozen incredible hiking tours ranging from 10 minutes to 4 hours. It was established in 1929.

The arches rise to a height of 112 feet and span 144 feet across. During the spring and fall season, crowds are minimal, allowing visitors to get excellent photos of this incredible view. Stargazing and nighttime photography are not only allowed, but encouraged. The park contains some of the darkest skies remaining in the 48 contiguous states, and park rangers host guide stargazing events regularly.

For backpackers who like to camp, Arches offers less than one dozen designated camp zones. These go quickly, so be sure to call months in advance in order to reserve or plan your trip.

Photo Credit: Alexandre Chambon (left), Lauren Pandolfi (below)

Badlands National Park contains
some of the most spectacular views
in South Dakota and is home to
bison, bighorn sheep, and prairie
dogs. For backpackers, the park is
ideal, as visitors are welcome to
camp anywhere in the 245,000
acre park.

Big Bend National Park, located in West Texas, is often noted for its harsh climate. However, despite hot and arid summers, the park contains a diversity of fauna and flora, including over 1,200 plant species and 4,200 animal species.

Photo Credit: Jesse Sewell

Biscayne National Park is largely comprised of underwater reefs home to over 200 species of fish, reptiles, mammals, and crustaceans. It is located on the southern tip of Florida.

Photo Credit: Shaun Wolfe

12

Black Canyon of the Gunnison National Park is so named because the lower parts of the canyon only receive a few minutes of sunlight each day. It has Colorado's steepest cliff, Painted Wall, which measures over 2,200 feet high.

Photo Credit: NPS

Bryce Canyon National Park, located in southwestern Utah, is a transcendental landscape marked by colorful, delicate pinnacles and large amphitheaters of rock. Over two million tourists visit the isolated park each year, utilizing the various one-day hiking trails and stunning scenic drive.

Bryce Canyon National Park offers two campgrounds, which are both located near the wondrous Bryce Amphitheater. North Campground is surrounded by Ponderosa Pine forest and is a comfortable distance from the Visitor Center. Sunset Campground is in close proximity to the Bryce Canyon Lodge and is also surrounded by Ponderosa Pine forest.

The best opportunities for sunrise photography are actually at Sunset Point (left). The most iconic rock formation is known as Thor's hammer, and is pictured below and left.

Photo Credit: Matt Noble (left), Drew Hays (below)

Canyonlands National Park, like Bryce Canyon, is located in Utah and contains similar rock formations caused by erosion. Mesa Arch (pictured here) is just one of many spectacular views at this rarely visited park.

Photo Credit: John Fowler

Capitol Reef is another national park that calls Utah home. Visitors often come for hiking, horseback riding, and photography. In addition to the rock formations, the park is unique for its shape, as it is over 60 miles long and only an average of 6 miles wide.

Photo Credit: Tracy Zhang

Carlsbad Caverns National Park, found along New Mexico's southern border with Texas, contains nearly 120 limestone caves and geological chambers. The cave systems are so far beneath the surface that elevators are required to take visitors up and down. Visitors are able to go on ranger-guided tours or obtain permits to do technical cave exploration.

Photo Credit: Dan Lang

Note: A disease called White-nose Syndrome is spreading through the United States, killing bat populations. In order to protect the bats at Carlsbad Caverns, all visitors who go into Carlsbad Cavern are required to walk the length of a bio-cleaning mat to remove spores and dirt after exiting the cavern.

Channel Islands National Park, off the
coast of southern California, receives
only around 300,000 visitors annually.
It is home to many aquatic mammals
and birds, as well as some sea caves,
which attract many sightseers.

Photo Credit: Jeremy Bishop

Congaree National Park is America's
largest remaining bottomland hardwood
forest, mostly consisting of cypress and
tupelo trees. Having one of the tallest
deciduous canopies in the world, birding
is especially popular, among other
activities, such as canoeing, hiking, and
camping.

Photo Credit: NPS

Crater Lake National Park is Oregon's only national park and is named after the deepest lake in America. This body of water has depths of nearly 2,000 feet and is a closed system, meaning there are no incoming or outgoing sources of water, other than evaporation and precipitation.

Photo Credit: Jeff Hopper

Cuyahoga Valley National Park, Ohio's only national park, was established in 2000. Most visitors go for trail-running, bicycling, and sightseeing at the historic buildings that were once used for mercantilism around the Erie Canal Towpath.

Photo Credit: Travis Essinger

Death Valley National Park is recognized as one of the world's hottest deserts. In spite of its heat, the park also contains incredible biodiversity and is home to bighorn sheep, burros, coyotes, bobcats, and more. Located in eastern California, Death Valley receives over one million visitors annually.

Photo Credit: Jakub Gorajek

Denali National Park, located in Central Alaska, is home to North America's tallest peak, Mount Denali, which rises to 20,310 feet. The park consists of a variety of geographical features, including forests, glaciers, and, of course, mountains.

Photo Credit: Lukas Ruzicka

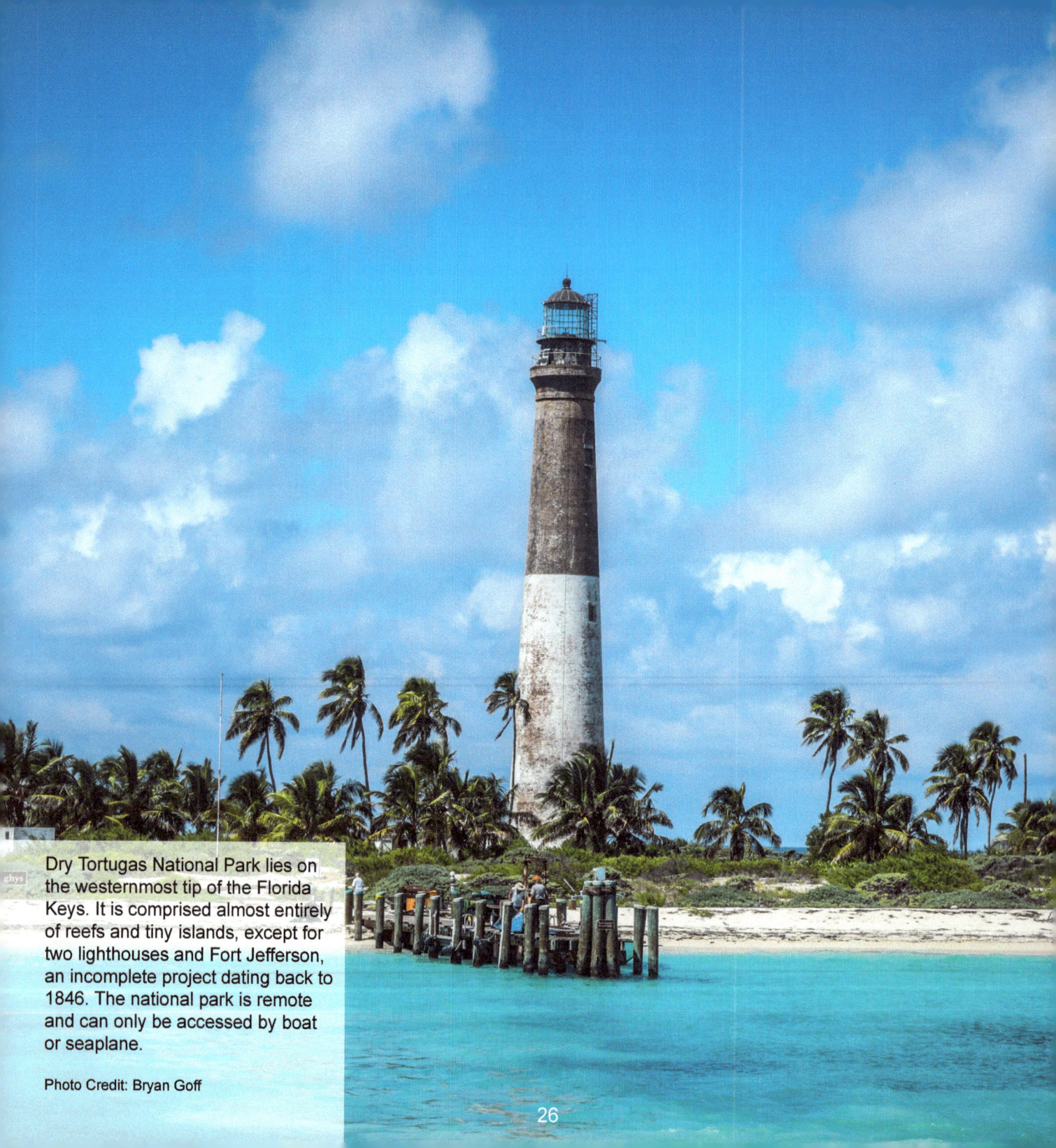

Dry Tortugas National Park lies on the westernmost tip of the Florida Keys. It is comprised almost entirely of reefs and tiny islands, except for two lighthouses and Fort Jefferson, an incomplete project dating back to 1846. The national park is remote and can only be accessed by boat or seaplane.

Photo Credit: Bryan Goff

Everglades National Park remains one of the most eco-diverse national parks in the U.S. On the southern tip of Florida, the park contains fresh-water sloughs, hardwood hammocks, pine rocklands, coastal lowlands, and estuaries. Much of the area, and the wildlife that inhabit it, are currently endangered.

Photo Credit: Tanja Cibulski

Gates of the Arctic National Park is the northernmost national park, and consists of over 13,000 square miles. Due to its location and lack of roads, Gates of the Arctic is the least visited of the 61 national parks in the U.S., with counts at around 10,000 people annually. Most visitors backpack and camp in the wilderness.

Photo Credit: Zach Richter

Established in February of 2018, Gateway Arch National Park is a relatively new member on the list of national parks. The monument itself is over 600 ft. in height and visitors are welcome to reserve tickets to ride a tram to the top. In addition to the Arch, the courthouse in which the Dred Scott case was tried is also on the grounds of the park.

Photo Credit: Logan Trxell (left), Joshua Ness (below)

Glacier National Park encompasses over one million acres of land in the northern region of Montana, and it contains more than 1,000 different species of plants. Over half of the park is forested, despite very cold and lengthy winters.

Photo Credit: Dan McCormick

Glacier Bay National Park lies along the southeastern Alaska coastline and is a common destination of cruise ships. It is home to one of the tallest coastal mountain ranges in the world, with numerous peaks reaching well over 10,000 feet.

Although the park is open year-round, actual services and available activities are quite limited during winter months. There are public roads that lead to Glacier Bay, and the Visitor Center is located at a small nearby basecamp called Bartlett Cove. Campsites, hiking, and water activities are all popular during peak season.

To visit the park, visitors must make arrangements to arrive via boat or plane. A variety of air-taxi and boating services are available, but plans must be made far in advance.

Below, a glacier calves, the name for when chunks of ice sheer off the face of a glacier.

Photo Credit: Richard Young (left), NPS (below)

Grand Canyon National Park is one of America's most iconic parks. More than 277 miles long, nearly 20 miles wide (in places) and a mile deep, the Grand Canyon draws over 6 million visitors a year.

Guests are welcome to hike any of the dozens of trails along both rims and into the canyon itself, however, hikers are cautioned about attempting the Down and Out Trail, as it is incredibly strenuous and can prove dangerous during the summer and winter seasons.

Despite the appearance of a desert landscape, the Grand Canyon is full of wildlife diversity. From mule dear and mountain lions, to tarantulas and scorpions, there are over 500 animal species in the park. The Canyon is a particular favorite of birdwatchers, as it is the home to over 355 varieties of birds.

Rich with history, views, and experiences, the Grand Canyon is an absolute must for anyone wishing to visit our natural national treasures.

Photo Credit: Matt Noble

Grand Teton National Park is set in beautiful northwestern Wyoming. The Teton Mountain peaks stay snowcapped year-round, but below the treeline, biodiversity abounds. Elk, moose, bear, deer, mountain lions, and even bighorn sheep are often seen by visitors.

Photo Credit: Brantley Childress

38

Great Basin National Park is most noted for the forests of ancient bristlecone pines, the oldest known nonclonal organisms. The park is located in Nevada.

Photo Credit: Frank Kovalchek

Great Sand Dunes National Park and Preserve in Colorado contains the tallest sand dunes in North America. They rise over 700 feet in height and cover an area of approximately 30 square miles.

Climbing the first dune places park visitors in a new world. Sand spreads for miles before you and beyond that, snow-capped mountains. If you hope to head to High Dune, you'll want to ensure several hours for the round trip. Dune climbers should also bring plenty of water, sunglasses, and a scarf, as sand can whip around quite heavily, and the sun can reflect off the sand.

The park is not just sand, however, and the diverse ecosystem supports over 250 bird species, dozens of fish and amphibian species, thousands of species of insects, not to mention bighorn sheep, marmots, black bears, mountain lions, elk, beavers, badgers, bison, and more.

Photo Credit: James Mertz (left), Matt Noble (above)

Great Smoky Mountains National Park straddles the border between North Carolina and Tennessee. In it, visitors can find lush forests and an abundance of wildflowers that bloom year-round. Over 11 million people go to the park annually.

Photo Credit: Ben Klea

Guadalupe Mountains National Park, in the vast Chihuahuan Desert of western Texas, is known for its bright white Salt Basin Dunes, wildlife-rich grassland and fossilized reef mountains. In the north, the McKittrick Canyon Trail is known for its colorful fall foliage.

Photo Credit: Miguel Vieira

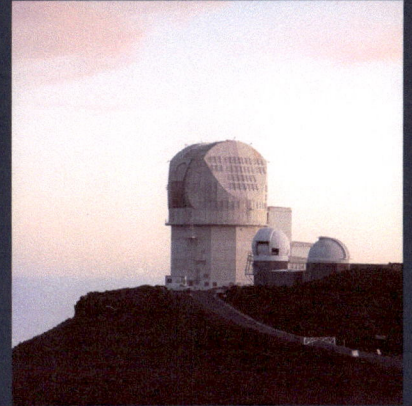

Haleakalā National Park, located on the island of Maui (the second largest Hawaiian Island), has peaks that reach over 10,000 feet above sea level. In the coastal region of Kīpahulu, the Pools of Ohe'o (freshwater pools and waterfalls) create beautiful juxtaposition to the volcanic aridity at higher elevations.

Hawaii has a long, and mostly unknown, history, though experts place polynesian settlers on the Island of Maui at least as early as A.D. 800. American settlement did not begin there until 1819, when missionaries and whalers arrived.

In 1898, Hawaii was annexed by the United States, and 18 years later, Hawai'i National Park was created (which, at the time, included Haleakala).

In 1935, a road was built to the summit, followed by cabins in 1937, and the Observatory in 1963.

Photo Credit: NOAA (left), Jad Limcaco

Hawai'i Volcanoes National Park contains two active volcanoes: Kīlauea, one of the world's most active volcanoes, and Mauna Loa, the world's largest shield volcano. Climates range from lush tropical rain forests to the arid and barren.

Photo Credit: Jack Ebnet

Hot Springs National Park was the
smallest national park in the United
States at just 5,550 acres, until the addition
of Gateway Arch National Park in 2018.
The northern slopes of the Arkansas ridges
and basins provide a suitable habitat
for a deciduous forest dominated by oak
and hickory.

Photo Credit: Yinan Chen

Indiana Dunes National Park is comprised of over 15,000 acres of shoreline along Lake Michigan. With nearly four million annual visitors, the park is already one of the most popular, despite being the newest addition to the national park list.

Isle Royale National Park is a remote island cluster in Lake Superior, near Michigan's border with Canada. The park is known for its wolf and moose populations.

Photo Credit: Ray Dumas

Joshua Tree National Park, named for California's bristly Joshua trees, includes the higher Mojave Desert and lower Colorado Desert. It is characterized by rugged rock formations and stark desert landscapes.

In 1918, a woman by the name of Minerva Hamilton Hoyt grew increasingly concerned about the deteriorating desert ecology. New roadways had brought increased vehicle traffic around and through the area that is now designated as Joshua Tree.

After founding and joining several national preservation organizations, Minerva lobbied for the State of California to protect three desert areas (Joshua Tree, Death Valley, and the Anza-Borrego Desert). In 1936, she won an ally in President Franklin D. Roosevelt, who made Joshua Tree a national monument.

In 1994, Joshua Tree's status was changed to national park and now, nearly three million visitors travel to the park every year. At the park, explorers can camp, hike, go birding, stargaze, rock climb, mountainbike, ride horseback, and more.

When planning a trip to the park, it is recommended to always consider the weather. During the winter, temperatures can drop into the 20s at night; in the summer, highs are almost always above 100 degrees. Such extremes require a good bit of planning.

Photo Credit: Elliott Engelmann

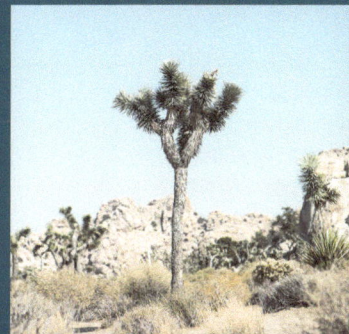

Katmai National Park in Alaska has hundreds of miles of coastline, vast regions of forest and tundra, lakes, rivers, small streams, and even several active volcanoes. The park is known for the many brown bears that are drawn to the salmon in the numerous waterways.

Photo Credit: Paxson Woelber

Kenai Fjords National Park, located along the southern coast of Alaska, contains the Harding Icefield, one of the largest ice fields in the United States. The park also has incredibly diverse wildlife populations, including bald eagles, black bears, and mountain goats.

Photo Credit: Phillip Sauerbeck (above), Daniel H. Tong (left)

Kings Canyon National Park, just
north of Sequoia National Park in
California, is known for its huge
sequoia trees, notably the enormous
General Grant Tree in Grant Grove.
The canyon expands outside the park
and is considered the deepest
in North America.

Photo Credit: Pablo Garcia Saldana

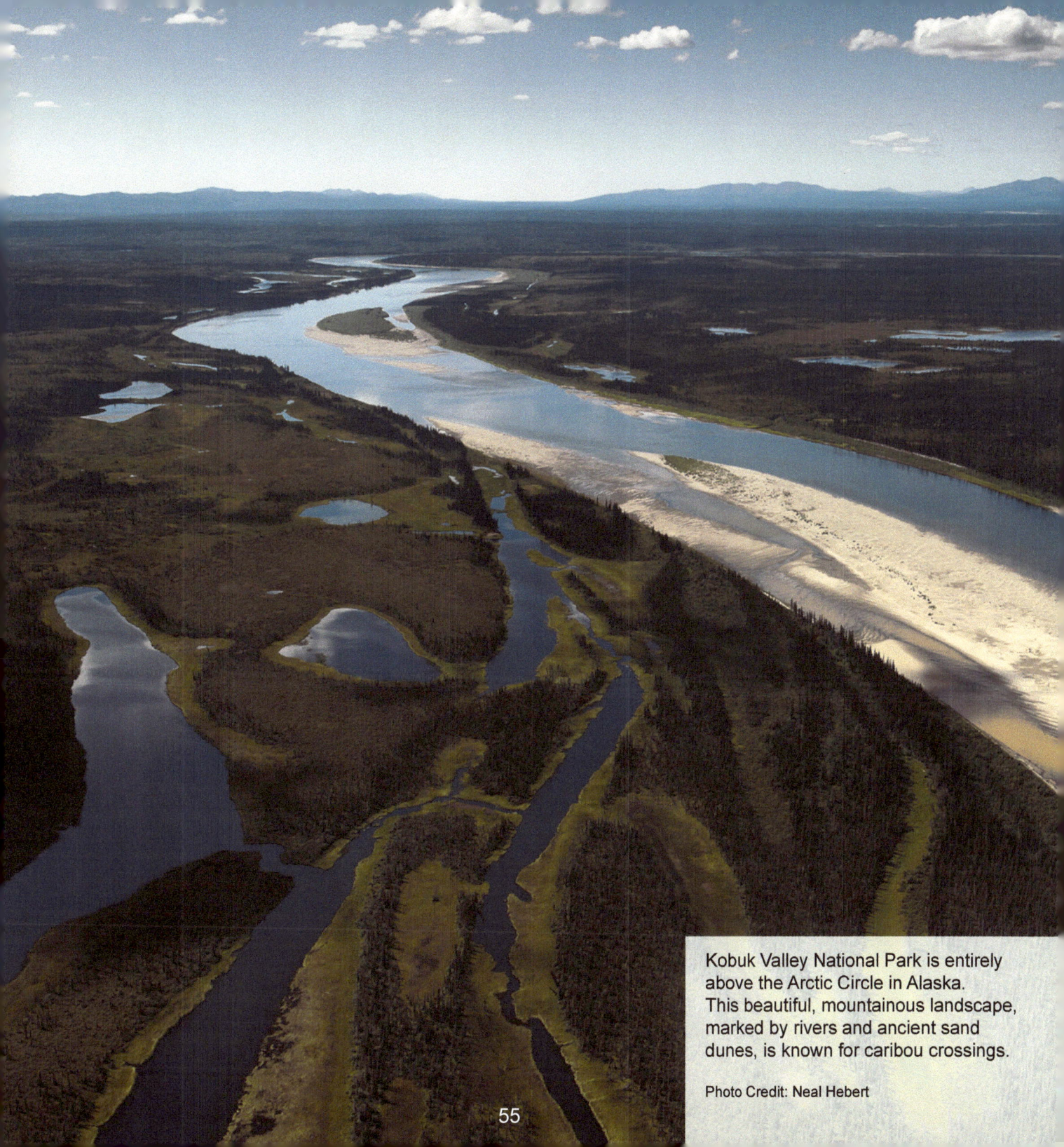

Kobuk Valley National Park is entirely above the Arctic Circle in Alaska. This beautiful, mountainous landscape, marked by rivers and ancient sand dunes, is known for caribou crossings.

Photo Credit: Neal Hebert

Lake Clark National Park, located in Alaska, is a frigid but gorgeous land of boreal forest and tundra. No roads lead in or out of the park, making it only accessible by floatplane, boat, or backpacking.

Photo Credit: Caitlin Marr

Lassen Volcanic National Park, located in northeastern California, is home to the world's largest plug dome volcano. The western part of the park features great lava pinnacles, jagged craters, and steaming sulfur vents.

Photo Credit: Patrick Bosigner (above), Hari Panicker (left)

Mammoth Cave National Park in Kentucky contains portions of Mammoth Cave, the longest cave system in the world. These caves are home to various species of bats, crickets, and salamanders.

Photo Credit: NPS

Mesa Verde National Park in southwest Colorado is known for its well-preserved Ancestral Puebloan cliff dwellings, notably the huge Cliff Palace. The park was named with the Spanish term for "green table" because of its forests of juniper and piñon trees, and it's flat-topped landforms.

Photo Credit: Daniel Holm Hansen

Mount Rainier National Park surrounds Mount Rainier, a 14,411-foot peak near Seattle, Washington. The park's 5,400-foot tall Paradise Valley offers mountain views, summertime wildflower meadows, and hiking trailheads.

Photo Credit: Christopher Burns

National Park of American Samoa spans three islands in the South Pacific. The surrounding waters are filled with a diversity of marine life, including sea turtles, humpback whales, nearly 1,000 species of fish, and over 250 coral species.

Photo Credit: Tavita Togia

61

North Cascades National Park is a vast wilderness of forested mountains, glaciers, and lakes in northern Washington State. The park shelters grizzly bears and gray wolves, plus more than 200 bird species.

Photo Credit: Justin Cron

Olympic National Park in Washington State sprawls across the Olympic Peninsula, west of Puget Sound. From dramatic peaks to old-growth forests, the park encompasses several different ecosystems. Within the center of Olympic National Park rise the Olympic Mountains, whose sides and ridgelines are topped with ancient glaciers.

Photo Credit: Sergei Akulich

Petrified Forest National Park in northeastern Arizona is home to the Rainbow Forest, which is full of colorful petrified wood (photo to the right). The Petrified Forest is also known for its fossils of animals from bygone eras.

Photo Credit: Scott Blake

Pinnacles National Park preserves a mountainous region located east of the Salinas Valley in central California. The park features unusual talus caves that house at least 13 species of bats.

Photo Credit: Daniel Hartwig

Redwood National Park, spread along the coast of northern California, protects nearly all of America's redwoods. One of its main attractions, Fern Canyon, contains seven different types of ancient ferns clinging to steep cliffs along a dirt path.

Photo Credit: Tara Schatz

Rocky Mountain National Park in north-central Colorado contains one of the most diverse fauna and flora habitats of the United States. Nearly five million people visit the park annually.

Photo Credit: Steve Enoch (above), Greg Amato (below)

Saguaro National Park delivers views of the Arizona desert landscape, which is said to contain nearly two million saguaro cacti. The park is home to some of America's most dangerous reptiles, including Gila monsters and six species of rattlesnakes.

Photo Credit: Lianda Ludwig

Sequoia National Park spans over 400,000 acres of Sierra Nevada in California, and contains over 8,000 sequoia trees. The park contains the highest point in the contiguous U.S., Mount Whitney, as well as the largest tree on earth, the General Sherman Tree.

Photo Credit: Susan Yin

Shenandoah National Park is a long, narrow park located in Virginia. It boasts numerous waterfalls, as well as many bird species, deer, squirrels, and black bears.

Theodore Roosevelt National Park in North Dakota is a perfect habitat for bison, elk, and prairie dogs. The park is known for the South Unit's colorful Painted Canyon.

Photo Credit: Jessica Rockeman (above), Richard Lee (left), Laure Thomas (right)

Virgin Islands National Park occupies the majority of St. John, one of the U.S. Virgin Islands. The park encompasses miles of hiking trails through the tropical rainforest and is also popular for scuba diving and snorkeling.

Photo Credit: Matt Wade (above), Vlad Tchompalov (left), Alex Perez (right)

Voyageurs National Park, located
in the northern reaches of Minnesota,
is one of the best locations in the
contiguous U.S. to view the Northern
Lights. The mainland area of the
park is only accessible by boat. During
winter, it's only accessible by
snowmobile, ski, or snowshoe.

Photo Credit: NPS/Steve Dimse

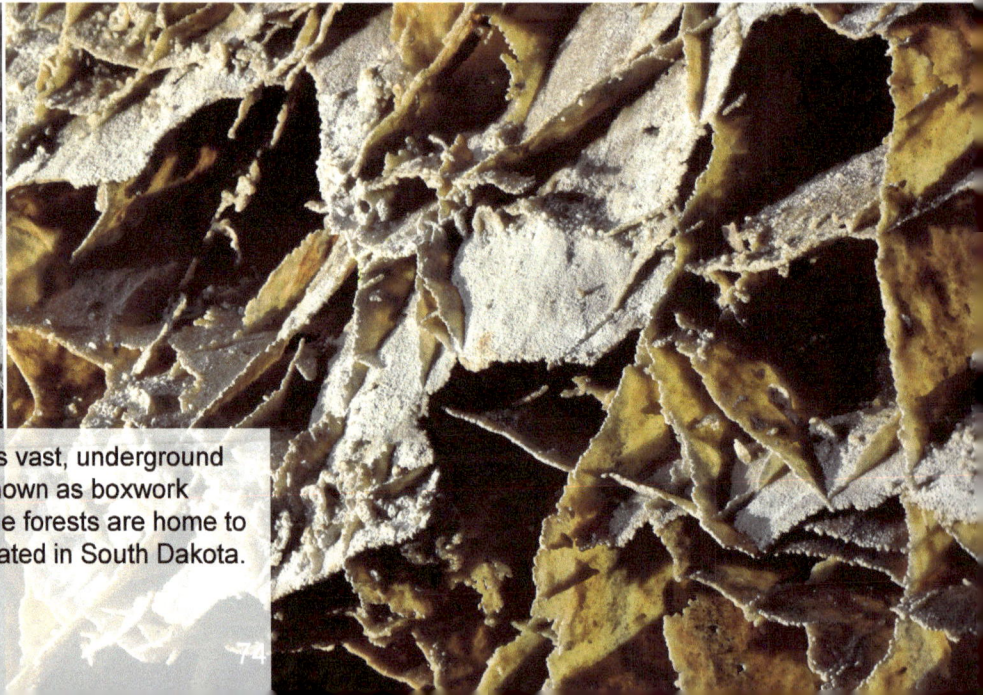

Wind Cave National Park is known for its vast, underground cave with distinct geologic formations known as boxwork and frostwork. The park's prairie and pine forests are home to bison, elk, and antelope. The park is located in South Dakota.

Photo Credit: NPS

Wrangell-St. Elias National Park, found in Alaska, forms the largest area (over 13 million acres) managed by the National Park Service. The park is home to Mount St. Elias, the second tallest mountain in North America.

Photo Credit: Brian Petrtyl (above), NPS (below)

Yellowstone was the first national park in the U.S. Spanning over an area larger than some U.S. states, it contains several well-known attractions, such as the Old Faithful geyser and Yellowstone Lake.

Photo Credit: Dmitry Sovyak

Yosemite National Park is nestled in the Sierra Nevada mountains of California and covers an area of 747,956 acres. It is home to the famed giant sequoia trees, El Capitan (one of the world's most popular rock climbing cliffs), and Half Dome, perhaps the most iconic peak in the national parks.

About five million visitors travel to Yosemite every year. With miles of trails, dozens of camp zones, waterfalls, rock climbing, fishing, horseback riding, stargazing, birding, and more, there are plenty of activities to keep anyone busy.

In June of 2017, Alex Honnold became the first person to free solo El Capitan, which means he climbed the cliff face by himself without any harnesses or safety equipment. The ascent took only four hours, though he spent years practicing and preparing.

At Half Dome, visitors are allowed to enter a lottery to be selected to receive a hiking permit to summit the peak. Below, you will find a picture of the backside of Half Dome, with hikers en route.

Photo Credit: Aniket Deole (left), Denys Nevozhai (below)

Zion National Park claims over 350 species of animals and 900 species of plants. Nestled in southern Utah, Zion attracts over five million visitors annually. The red cliffs (seen left) offer excellent rockclimbing. The Narrows (below) are miles of water hiking, and the lack of light pollution provides excellent stargazing (seen above).

Photo Credit: Matt Noble (left), Natalie Chaney (above), Karan Chawla (below)

www.ingramcontent.com/pod-product-compliance
Lightning Source LLC
Chambersburg PA
CBHW060933150426
42812CB00060B/2636